·SUN·
·MOON·
·AND·
STARS·

BY

MARY HOFFMAN

AND

JANE RAY

Orion
Children's Books

For our friend and editor Judith Elliott,
who looked up at the night sky and saw this book

First published in Great Britain in 1998
by Orion Children's Books
a division of the Orion Publishing Group Ltd
Orion House
5 Upper St Martin's Lane
London WC2H 9EA

Text copyright © Mary Hoffman 1998
Illustrations copyright © Jane Ray 1998
Designed by Ian Butterworth

A catalogue record for this book is available from the British Library
Printed in Italy
ISBN 1 85881 413 8

Introduction

The sky is a vast storybook open above us. But it doesn't tell the same stories to everyone. For thousands of years, people have looked up at it, by day and by night, and taken from it the tales that explained some of the amazing things they saw there.

By day the sky can be made so bright by the sun that we can't look at it. In other parts of the world the sun seems to depart for an endless winter. Each brings about its own set of stories. By night, a clear sky is full of events and characters – a living collection of tales just waiting to be told.

Thousands of years ago people's view of the night sky was clear, because there were no artificial lights in the streets powerful enough to outshine the stars. And there were no strong artificial lights in their homes either, so they went to bed when it got dark and got up when the sun rose again.

People of the ancient world made up stories to explain what they could see in the sky by day and night; some of these stories we still know and call them the myths and legends of different cultures.

The stories and beliefs gathered together here form a window to the imagination of people who did not know the explanations of the natural world that we take for granted today. We all share a desire to explain things in terms of what we see with our own eyes. Even though we know today that the moon stays the same size and shape all the time, we still talk about "a full moon" or "a crescent moon". We know that the sun stays in the same place while the earth goes around it, yet we still use words like "sunrise" and "sunset".

Mythology isn't bad science; it is something quite different. Through these ancient stories we learn something about the human mind, and with it something about ourselves. Scientific truth is not the only kind. Who knows what stories we might make up to explain what we see in sky, if we had nothing to go on but the evidence of our eyes? The appearance and movement of the sun, moon and stars will continue to fascinate and inspire us till the end of time.

Contents

Introduction 7

SKY

Reading the sky 12

The giant's skull (a Norse myth) 14

Mother sky (an Egyptian myth) 6

A handful of quartz (a Navajo myth) 18

Days of old 20

War in heaven (Latvian myths) 22

The king's fire dogs (a Korean myth) 24

SUN

Temples of the sun 26

The heavenly archer (a Chinese legend) 28

The fifth sun (a Mayan myth) 30

When the sun hid (a Japanese myth) 32

Sunlore 34

In the sun's house (a Navajo myth) 36

Phaëton's Last Ride (a Greek legend) 40

MOON

Crying for the moon 44

Anancy and the Flipflap bird (an Afro-Caribbean legend) 46

The drowned moon (an English legend) 48

The woman who flew to the moon (a Chinese legend) 50

Moonlore 52

The hare in the moon (a Hindu legend) 54

Moonchildren (a Norse myth) 56

The cheese in the pond (an English folktale) 58

STARS

The circle of beasts (Zodiac myths) 60

Seven sisters (an Australian myth) 64

The divided lovers (a Japanese myth) 66

Starlore 68

The price of vanity (a Greek myth) 70

White Star Woman and Great Star (a Pawnee myth) 72

About the stories 74

SKY

Reading the sky

The sky is not just a storybook.
For thousands of years it also provided the most reliable map there was.

Sailors used to navigate by the stars, using an instrument called an astrolabe. The most important star for them was the North Star or Pole Star. In the ancient world, sailors believed that the Pole Star was fixed so all the other stars could be positioned in relation to it like horses tethered to a stake.

Until the Polish astronomer
Copernicus first worked out in 1510
that the earth went round the sun, people
thought that the earth was the centre of the
universe and the sun travelled round it. This
didn't stop them from orienting their
journeys by the sun's rising in the East and
setting in the West. The word "orient"
comes from the Latin "sol oriens",
the sun rising.

And people went on believing that the earth was flat until Christopher Columbus travelled to America, even though it had been suggested by the Greeks at least two thousand years earlier that it was round. It just seemed too hard to believe when mariners and other travellers regularly saw the sun "rise" and "sink" above and below the flat horizon every day.

The giant's skull

IN THE BEGINNING THERE WERE TWO PLACES — A LAND OF FIRE AND A LAND OF ICE. In the void between them there was just one huge creature – Ymir. He was an evil frost giant and he was hungry. But there was nothing to eat because he was living in nothingness. Gradually he saw another figure taking shape in the gloom. It was the great cow Audumla. Milk was flowing from her in four streams, so Ymir was able to satisfy his hunger. Then he fell into a deep sleep.

But Audumla was hungry too and started to lick the salty blocks of ice. At the end of the first day, a man's head had appeared; two days later a complete man sprang out of the ice. This first man was called Buri and he hated Ymir.

In time Buri had sons and grandsons, who became the gods who made the world. Led by Odin the chief god, they killed Ymir and looked at his enormous body. They took his mighty skull and fixed it up above the earth to make the dome of the sky. It reached down at the four corners of East, South, West and North. The earth itself they made by grinding up Ymir's flesh, turning his bones into mountains and his blood into the seas.

At that time the sky was still dark. Odin and his brothers took sparks from Muspel, the land of fire, and threw them into the heavens. They became the stars and from that day to this they have travelled the paths through the sky that Odin gave them to follow. There were two fire-flakes bigger than all the rest and the gods chose them to be the sun and moon. Then the gods had golden chariots made by their smiths, to drive the sun and moon on their paths across the sky. And this is how the lights of heaven were made, all held inside the dome of the giant's skull.

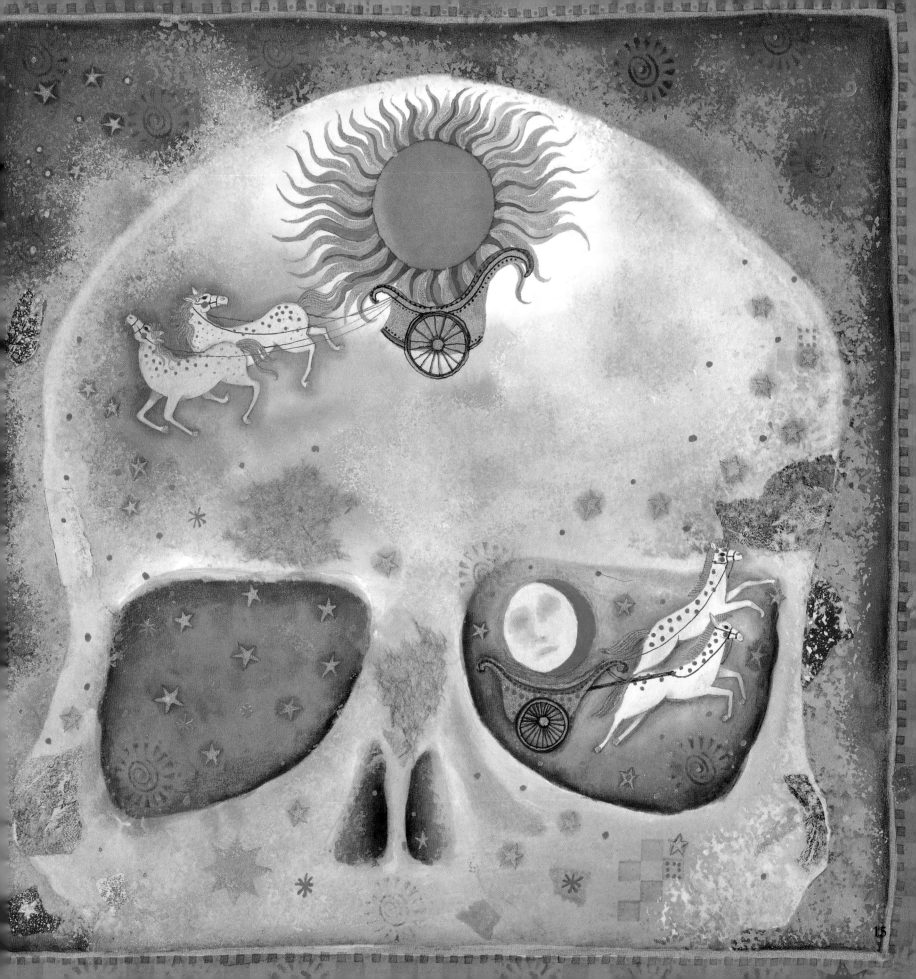

16

Mother sky

THE EGYPTIAN UNIVERSE BEGAN IN WATER AND DARKNESS. Atum, the first sungod, created himself on a mound that rose out of the water. Atum spluttered as he emerged from the mud and stood upright. He sneezed and his son Shu was born. Atum spat to clear his throat and out came his daughter Tefnut.

The twins Shu and Tefnut were part human and part lion. They themselves had twins, Nut and Geb, who became the sky and the earth. Nut was the sky goddess. She stretched her great body across the world and it was covered by the stars, who were just some of her many children. Geb, whose body made the earth, had four children with Nut and then Shu, their father, separated them with his strong arms.

Helped by the winds, mighty Shu keeps Nut stretched above the world so that the heavens will not fall on those who live beneath the starry arch of her body. Beyond her is the water of creation, which she also keeps away from the earth. Her feet are planted in the east and her hands in the west.

The sungod of the Egyptians has many names and personalities. As Ra he sails up and across the underside of his mother Nut's body every day in a boat. At the end of the day, when Ra's boat reaches the West, Nut swallows him and he is lost to the world.

Every morning Nut gives birth to the sun god again and he sets off in a different boat back across the sky, which is his mother's belly. When Egyptians died, they believed they would live on in the stars, so the inside of their coffin-lids often had a painting of Nut stretching her starry body over the dead.

A handful of quartz

IN THE FIFTH WORLD, WHICH IS THE ONE WE LIVE IN, THERE WERE FOUR LIGHTS: WHITE IN THE EAST, BLUE IN THE SOUTH, YELLOW IN THE WEST, AND BLACK — THE LIGHT THAT IS DARKNESS — WHICH SPREAD FROM THE NORTH.

The people all complained that they hadn't got enough light to see and work by, so First Woman came up with a plan. She took a huge slab of quartz and set it on a blanket, where she and her helpers cut out two large circles from the stone.

The first one they decorated with turquoise and red coral and feathers from four of their native birds — the cardinal, flicker, lark and eagle. They wanted to place it in the sky, so Fire Man suggested carrying it to the top of the highest mountain, where it was fastened to the sky with darts of zigzag lightning.

The second circle was supposed to carry coolness, so they decorated it with white shell and yellow pollen and gave it the feathers of the magpie, nighthawk, turkey and crane. This one they took to another mountain and fastened this one with sheet lightning.

But the trouble was that this first sun and moon were just stones and couldn't move. Then two wise old men offered to give up their spirits and give life to the quartz circles. So one entered the turquoise disc and became Sunbearer, and the other entered the white disc and became Moonbearer.

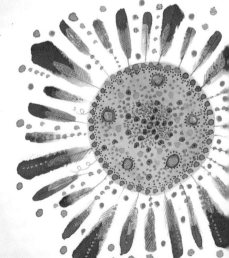

The people were now content. But First
Woman still had lots of chippings of quartz left over.
She carefully fashioned them into stars - the Pole Star, the
Cold Man of the North, Thunderbird and all the others -
and Fire Man climbed his ladder and placed them carefully
in their right places in the sky.

But Coyote wanted to help and he was not a patient
animal. First Woman gave him some stars to place, but he
soon got tired of climbing up the ladder to the sky. So he
took two corners of the blanket and tossed all the
remaining chips of quartz up into the heavens. They made
a great arc from horizon to horizon and that is how the
Milky Way was formed.

Days of old

As well as being a storybook and a map, the sky gives us our calendar.

The main thing about the sky is the way it gives us a measurable day – the hours of daylight provided by the sun. But the day is not the same length all the year round. The only time it is the same length as the night is at the two "equinoxes" which come in late March and late September. The longest day comes in late June and the shortest in late December at the two "solstices" when the sun appears to stand still.

This divides the year handily into four sections, which correspond to the beginning of the four seasons.

People observed that the moon apparently changed shape, from a thin new moon through to a full one, followed by a few days of no moon at all, in a regular pattern of twenty-eight days. That gave us a month, which comes from the Anglo-Saxon word for moon.

The year, of 365 days and a quarter, is the time it takes for the earth to go round the sun. But it wasn't until Julius Caesar's time, when people still believed that the sun went round the earth, that this was worked out. Caesar invented the calendar we still basically use, with a year of 365 days and one extra day every four years in a "Leap Year". In 1582 Pope Gregory XIII, to make up for the fact that the year is about eleven minutes shorter than 365 days and a quarter, added the rule that century years should be Leap Years only when they could be divided by 400.

The only part of the calendar not based on the movement of heavenly bodies is the week. But even its days are named after the sun (Sunday), moon (Monday) and the planet Saturn (Saturday). In other European languages, all the other days of the week are named after planets too, like Martedi, Italian for Tuesday, which is named for Mars.

SPRING

APRIL

MARCH · ARIES · TAURUS · MAY

PISCES EQUINOX AQUARIUS

FEBRUARY

JANUARY

CAPRICORN SOLSTICE

DECEMBER SAGITTARIUS

NOVEMBER SCORPIO

AUTUMN

GEMINI · JUNE

SOLSTICE · CANCER · JULY

SUMMER

LEO · AUGUST

VIRGO · SEPTEMBER

LIBRA EQUINOX OCTOBER

21

War in heaven

THE PEOPLE OF EASTERN EUROPE HAD A SUN GODDESS THEY WERE VERY FOND OF. Her name was Saule and her worshippers called her "dear little red sun". She was a motherly protector of orphans and took care of all her people, even helping shepherds to search if they lost a lamb.

Saule crosses the sky every day in a sledge drawn by two horses of pure gold; at night she rests on an island of apples in the West, but not before washing down her horses on the seashore. By the morning, helped by her many daughters, Saule and her horses have swum through the night sea and are ready to start their journey again.

Saule has several husbands; one of them is Meness, the warrior of the moon. He is handsome, dark and princely, wearing a cloak covered in stars. He drives a sledge pulled by black horses, travelling through the heavens at Saule's side.

One night, when Meness went to count the stars, which was his job, he found there was one missing. It was Auseklis, the morning star, and Meness was immediately suspicious. "He is in Germany, making gold coins", said the other stars, but Meness was sure that the morning star was with Saule. Immediately he went and stole Auseklis' fiancée, who was one of Saule's own bright daughters.

When Saule found out the double treachery, she was furious. She took a great sword and cut the moon in pieces. Her sun-maiden daughter took pity on Meness and put him back together again, but that is why we see different pieces of the moon at different times of the month. After that, Saule would never travel with Meness again. They divorced and Meness has the night sky for his kingdom and has to make do with that, for Saule will have none of him in the bright sky of daytime.

23

The king's fire dogs

HEAVEN CONTAINS JUST AS MANY COUNTRIES AS THE EARTH DOES. In the Land of Darkness there is a king who keeps huge fierce dogs. This king is always trying to think of ways to bring more light to his country.

One day, he called the biggest and most ferocious of his fire dogs and told it to go and bring him the sun. Off loped the dog and tried to seize the sun in his jaws. But the sun was so hot that it burnt his mouth. He snapped at it again and again, but could not hold on. He had to go back to his master with his tail between his legs.

The king summoned his next biggest dog. He sent it to steal the moon for him, thinking that it wouldn't be as hot as the sun, so his dog should be able to bring it back to him. But the second dog fared no better than the first. The moon was so cold that when he tried to bite it, it froze the dog's tongue to his mouth and made his teeth sing with pain. Hard as he tried, he could not hang on to the moon and had to spit it out. He slunk back to the king.

The king of darkness never gives up hope and every now and then he sends one of his fire dogs to try and steal the sun or the moon. You can see the bite marks whenever there's an eclipse.

SUN

25

Temples of the sun

All over the world, people have worshipped the sun as a powerful god or goddess. And they have built places of worship in the sun's honour.

In Ancient Egypt the burial chambers of the kings were placed in huge pyramids. The tip of the pyramid was plated with gold and was associated with the sun. Outside the pyramid a temple was built on the East side, where the sun rose, for worship of the dead king, who became the son of Ra, the sungod.

In South
America the
Mayans made their own
kind of pyramids for sun
worship. The one at Teotihucán is
called The Pyramid of the Sun. The Mayans
and Aztecs used to sacrifice people in the belief
that the sun needed blood in order to keep moving.

There may have been human sacrifice at Stonehenge too. These massive stones are arranged in a circle in such a way that the sun, rising on dawn midsummer's day, appears directly above the Heel Stone outside the mouth of the inner ring of stones.

Roman temples of the sungod Mithras, whose cult came from what is now Iran, were built underground in cave-like places. But there would be a hole pierced in the roof to let the sun's rays in.

The heavenly archer

FTER P'AN KU, THE CREATOR, PLACED THE SUN AND MOON IN THE SKY, THEY KEPT THEIR APPOINTED PLACES. BUT THERE CAME A TIME WHEN TERRIBLE DISASTERS OVERTOOK THE SKY AND THE LAND. Ten suns appeared in the sky and a monstrous snake devoured hundreds of people. The Emperor called for his best archer Sheng I, and sent him to deal with the monster.

Sheng I found that the real cause of the trouble was nine birds standing on three mountains, who were breathing out fire and causing nine false suns to burn in the sky. Sheng I shot all nine birds and the false suns dissolved into red clouds, leaving the true sun shining.

At about the same time, the Emperor saw a trail of light blaze across the sky and sent Sheng I to investigate. The fearless archer mounted the streak of shining air as if it were a horse and travelled where it took him. It was actually the wake of a fiery dragon, who was carrying one of the immortals to visit her mother, the goddess of the West Wind.

The goddess had heard that Sheng I was not just a mighty archer but a skilled architect. She asked him to build her a new palace and in return she promised him the secret potion of immortality. Who can resist the idea of eternal life? So Sheng I built the goddess a wonderful new palace of jade and glass and she gave him the potion.

The goddess's husband told Sheng I that he deserved a reward for shooting the nine false suns and gave him a new home in the sun. He also gave him a bird with real gold feathers who would teach him how to steer the sun through the heavens, making it keep its proper path which gives the earth the seasons.

So Sheng I built a magnificent palace for himself in the sun and has lived there ever since.

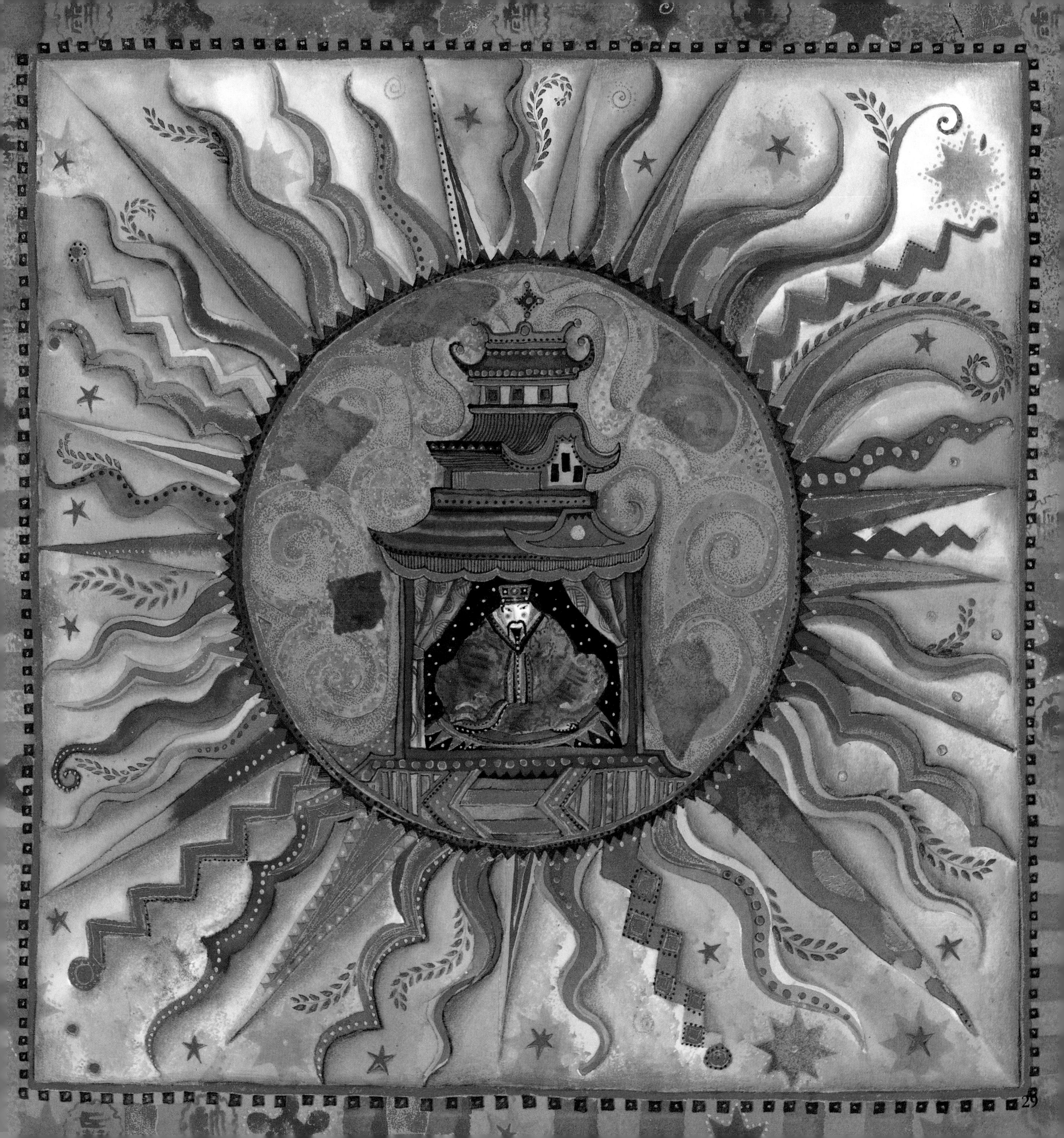

The fifth sun

For the Aztecs of old Mexico, there were four worlds before this one was created, each lit by its own sun. There was the sun of giants, the sun of wind, the sun of rain and the sun of water, under whose rule the earth was destroyed by a great flood. After that, the gods made a new earth and filled it with people, animals and plants.

The gods gathered together in the dark to decide how to make a fifth and last sun. They decided that one of them must give his life to become the sun, and asked for volunteers. Two gods said they would do it. One was the proud and boastful Tecuciztecatl and the other was the humble Nanahuatzin, who was suffering from a disease.

When the time came for the sacrifice, Tecuciztecatl was splendidly dressed in gold cloth, wearing beads of jade and coral. Nanahuatzin had on a robe made of paper. The rest of the gods gathered round a huge fire which had been burning for four days and urged Tecuciztecatl to jump in. But the vain god was all talk and no action. Four times he ran towards the flames and four times stopped at the very edge of the fire.

Then the gods were angry and called on Nanahuatzin. He did not hesitate for a second but ran straight into the heart of the flames. Immediately he was burned to a crisp. Shamed by the courage of his rival, Tecuciztecatl at last braved the fire himself, and he too was killed.

The gods all looked up to the sky, which was turning a magnificent red. Up over the eastern horizon sailed

Nanahuatzin, no longer a poor and diseased figure, but the splendid sun, shooting out rays of dazzling light over the earth. The gods renamed him Tonatiuh and he was the fifth sun.

But what was this? Another light, as bright as Tonatiuh was rising in the east. It was Tecuciztecatl, the proud but cowardly god. The others thought the earth would be too bright with two suns, so one of them threw a rabbit in Tecuciztecatl's face. This made him dimmer and he became the moon. At full moon you can still see the rabbit on his face.

Now there was a sun and moon but they were motionless. All the other gods had to die in order for the sun to move across the sky and that is how the fifth sun became the one we still see today.

When the sun hid

IN JAPAN THERE WAS A SUN GODDESS CALLED AMATERASU, WHO WAS SO BEAUTIFUL AND SO BRIGHT THAT HER PARENTS, WHO MADE THE WORLD, GAVE HER THE SKY TO BE HER HOME. But she had a wicked younger brother, Susanowo, who delighted in plaguing and tormenting the other gods. He was supposed to be in charge of weather and fertility, but he was lazy and very envious of his sister.

When Susanowo told Amaterasu that he was coming on a visit, the sun goddess was immediately suspicious. She dressed herself as a warrior, with her hair plaited and adorned with jewels. She carried a huge bow and a quiver that held a thousand arrows.

"What's this?" said Susanowo, grinning sarcastically. "Aren't you pleased to see me, sister?" And then he stormed into her rice-fields and destroyed all her crops. But worse was to come. Later, while Amaterasu and her women were weaving, Susanowo killed a horse and skinned it and threw its corpse into the weaving room.

That was too much for Amaterasu. She gathered her shining robes about her, descended gracefully from the blue sky and entered a cave, whose door she firmly fastened. This was a catastrophe. All life on earth came to a standstill and even the gods fell into a depression. Something had to be done.

So the god of Thought made a plan. The gods took lots of stars and welded them together to make a mirror. They brought a tree decorated with jewels and ribbons and placed it outside the cave; they hung the shining mirror in its branches.

Then came Ame-no-uzume, goddess of joy, and began a noisy dance, beating on a tub. Wilder and wilder became her dance, and more and more undignified, till all the gods were laughing and making such a noise that Amaterasu opened the cave door a crack to see what was going on. Immediately the gods put the mirror outside the door and the sun goddess saw her own dazzling reflection. "Who is this imposter?" she cried, flinging the door open wide. The gods pounced and bound her with a rope and carried her back to heaven. The cave was sealed and Amaterasu has stayed in the sky ever since.

Sunlore

There are all sorts of superstitions, sayings and traditions connected with the sun.

There is a very old belief that if you get up very early on the morning of Easter Day, you will see the sun dancing as it rises up in the East.

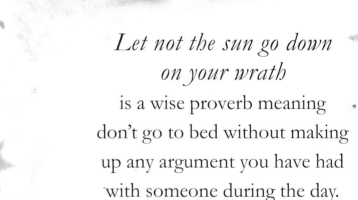

Let not the sun go down on your wrath is a wise proverb meaning don't go to bed without making up any argument you have had with someone during the day.

If you get up early on Mayday (the first of May) and wash your face in the dew at sunrise, you will have a beautiful complexion.

Make hay while the sun shines

means have fun while you can (tomorrow it may rain).

Sunwise is the same movement as clockwise. It is the favourable direction in which to progress.

The opposite, counter-clockwise, is "Widdershins" considered very unlucky and associated with evil arts.

One plate serves the whole world

Serbo-Croatian riddle.

Holding a candle to the sun

means making a feeble attempt to compete with something or someone way above our level.

In the sun's house

Changing Woman was the daughter of darkness and dawn, but she was brought up by First Man and First Woman. They fed her on nothing but pollen and dew, until she was a young woman. She changed with the seasons, but she was always beautiful. One hot day, she fell asleep out in the open when the sun was high in the sky. When she awoke, she felt hot and tired and she could see a trail of big footprints coming to her from the East and going away again.

After two days Changing Woman began to feel unwell, and two days later she gave birth to a baby boy. She hid the baby and went to wash herself in a pool. She let the water fall on her from a fresh stream and then went home. Two days later she felt unwell again and two days after that, Changing Woman gave birth to another baby boy.

These were miraculous children, who could walk in four days, and they grew like wild corn. The people needed heroes then, because there was a plague of monsters killing and eating everyone they could get hold of. The worst one, and chief of all the monsters, was Yeitso, Big Giant.

By the time Changing Woman's sons were twelve years old, they were strapping young men who could use a bow and arrow, and they were determined to find their father and kill Big Giant. They crept out of the hogan one day while their mother was asleep and set off on their quest, travelling eastwards.

37

The twins, who had no names as yet, stepped on to a cloud and then travelled up into the sky along a rainbow. Theirs was a long journey and they faced many dangers on the way, but they also met people who wanted to help them. One was Spider Woman. She made the older brother eat a piece of turquoise and the younger a piece of white shell. She gave them both an eagle feather and said "keep these close to your heart and don't show your father. I stole them from him."

After a long time they saw the Sun's house in the distance. It was guarded by four bears, four snakes, four winds and four thunders. The twins were scared, but went in all the same. The Sun was out on his journeys, but his daughter helped them to hide. When the Sun got back he put the boys through many tests to see if they were really children of his. They would have died if they hadn't had the eagle feathers hidden near their hearts.

At last the Sun agreed that they were his offspring and he gave them their names. The older boy he called Monster-Slayer and the younger Born-for-Water. He opened the doors in the four sides of his house, doors of turquoise, white shell, abalone and jet, and offered them anything they could see through them. But all the twins wanted was weapons and armour so that they could kill Big Giant.

The Sun made the twins stand on two buffalo hides, and then gave them armour and weapons made of flint. When they were ready, the Sun stood them on a flash of lightning and fired them at the earth, so that they landed near the lake where Big Giant came to drink.

Down to the water lumbered the fearful monster, to slake his thirst after a day of eating people. When he caught sight of the twins, he shot four arrows made of zigzag lightning at them. But Monster-Slayer and Born-for-Water caught the arrows and shot them back at Big Giant, piercing his heart on both sides. He crashed to the ground, then rose and fell again, each time in a new direction. When he fell for the fifth time, facing north-east he didn't get up. The Sun watched the battle from the sky. He knew that Big Giant had to die, but he was also one of the Sun's children.

Monster-Slayer and Born-for-Water returned in triumph to their mother's hogan, singing all the way. She was so proud of them she wept for joy, and so did all the other people, at least those that were left.

Phaëton's last ride

The Greek sungod had many names – he was called Helios, Phoebus and Apollo. One of his nicknames was Phaëton; it means "the Shining" and he gave it to his son by Clymene. She later married a mortal man, but Phaëton always knew that his real father was special. Like many boys with absent fathers, he would boast to his friends, only these boasts were way over the top.

"My father carries the sun across the heavens every day in a burning chariot drawn by four fiery horses," he would say. "They travel in a burnished bowl from East to West."

This did not make Phaëton popular and in the end one young man of his age was so tired of this story that he said, "If your father is the sungod, prove it!"

Phaëton went to his mother, and she sent him to the palace of the Sun. Phoebus was amazed when he saw his son for the first time. He was radiantly beautiful, with hair the colour of sunrise and eyes as blue as the heavens. He strode fearlessly enough up to his father's throne, but he had to shield his eyes from the glory of the sungod's presence.

Phaëton demanded some proof to show the world he was Phoebus' son. The god agreed but, to his horror he discovered that Phaëton wanted to drive the chariot of the sun! Sadly he led his son out to the stables where the four fiery horses tossed their manes and had them harnessed to the chariot.

41

Phoebus smeared his son's face with an ointment to protect him from the fierce rays of the sun.

"Do not urge the horses on," he warned. "Always rein them back." But it was no use.

The horses knew straightaway that someone lighter and less strong than their usual driver held the reins. They galloped out of control across the heavens, sometimes too high, leaving lands cold and streams frozen, sometimes too low, scorching the earth into deserts and drying up rivers. Mother Earth herself cried out to Zeus, the leader of the gods, for mercy.

Zeus sighed and aimed a bolt of lightning at the young charioteer and Phaëton fell to his death in the river Po in Italy. His mourning sisters were turned into poplar trees and their tears became the amber that Roman girls wore as wedding jewellery.

As for Phoebus, he grieved so much for his golden child that the sun went into eclipse for three days. But in the end he had to admit that Zeus could have done nothing else. He took up the reins again. The Shining was dimmed for ever, but the world still needed light.

MOON

Crying for the moon

Just as the sun is associated with life and energy, so the moon has been connected with death and disaster. Perhaps because it seems to have horns when it is crescent, it has been associated with the devil. This may be why legends of werewolves and vampires suggest that these gruesome transformations take place at full moon.

The moon is also associated with water, since it is the force of the moon's gravity which pulls large bodies of water, causing the tides of the earth's seas and oceans.

Anancy and the Flipflap bird

Anancy, the spiderman, had six children. Their names were See All, Roadbuilder, Riverdrinker, Fishcutter, Stonethrower and Cushion, and if you can't guess why, well, this story will tell you.

One day, Anancy had to go to town on business, so he kissed his children goodbye and set off. Soon afterwards, See All called the others together and said "Quick! Father is in danger. He has fallen in the river and been swallowed by a fish!"

Roadbuilder immediately made a path with his spider silk and they all travelled on it to the river. Riverdrinker swallowed up all the water in one big gulp and Fishcutter split open the fish. But Anancy's adventures were not over yet, for the great Flipflap bird swooped down and caught him up in her beak.

Stonethrower quickly scooped up a pebble and hit the bird on the wing so that she opened her beak to squawk. Cushion darted back and forth as Anancy fell, positioning herself perfectly to soften his landing.

After so much excitement, they all went home, the children arguing on the way which of them had been most useful. When they arrived home Anancy took a turn in the garden. He wanted to think of a reward he could give the children, who had certainly saved his life. Suddenly he spotted a large glowing ball behind his avocado tree.

"Just the thing!" thought Anancy. "What a pity there is only one of it." He went indoors and asked the children who should have the prize.

"Me, of course," said See All. "If it weren't for me, no-one would have known Father was in danger."

"Nonsense!" said Roadbuilder ...

And so it went on, with each child claiming the prize. Meanwhile, the Flipflap bird had turned up in the garden. Her wing was still sore from being hit by the pebble, and she had lost her lunch when she dropped Anancy. She spotted the glowing ball and thought she would play a trick on the spider family. Groaning at the weight, she picked up the ball in her beak and carried it as high in the sky as she could. At last she hung it on the tip of a star.

Anancy went back out into the garden, but the ball had disappeared! He searched everywhere before he realised that it was hanging up in the sky. He went in and brought his children out. "Let that be an end to the argument," he said. "I have hung the ball in the sky so that you can all share it. It will give light to the world every night, and I shall call it the moon."

His children thought Anancy had been very clever, but See All knew what had really happened. She said nothing and the moon is still up there, thanks to the Flipflap bird.

The drowned moon

Long ago when East Anglia was all bogs and marshes, the moon was shining up in the sky, just the way she does now, lighting up the marsh-pools. So you could walk about, picking your way as safely as by daylight. But when the moon was on the wane, and the skies were dark, out came all the slimy creeping evil creatures like bogles and will o' the wisps, who lured people to their deaths.

The moon was upset when she heard this, and decided to come down to earth to see for herself. So she wrapped her radiance in a black velvet cloak and stepped down from the sky, right on to the edge of the marshes. There was no light except from the glimmer of her silvery white feet as she threaded her way through the stagnant pools.

And all at once, she missed her footing and slipped and fell into the murky water. Swift as lightning, the marsh-bogles and fen-boggarts were upon her, tangling her up in the slimy roots of water-plants. Struggle as she would, she could not get free.

A traveller was picking his way across the marshes when suddenly the moon's hood fell back from her face and her glorious light streamed out over the water. He gave thanks that he had been saved and hastily made his way home, giving no thought to where the light came from.

Meanwhile the evil marsh creatures pushed the moon under the water and placed a great stone over her. Some days later, when everyone was wondering where the new moon had got to, the traveller remembered how he had been helped.

"I think I know where the moon is," he exclaimed. "She may have drowned in the marshes." A group of villagers got together with ropes and lanterns and set out for the marshes. The rescued traveller showed them the way, and they found a huge stone sticking out of the water.

They all heaved and strained until they had lifted the stone out. Immediately a beautiful silver face floated to the top of the water and in a brilliant and dazzling display of light the drowned moon rose up out of the marshes and sailed back up to the sky. Since then she has shone as brightly as she can over the marshes, to keep the bogles away.

49

The woman who flew to the moon

Heng O was the beautiful sister of a water god. She was married to Sheng I, the archer who shot the nine false suns, and they were very happy. But one day Heng O discovered that her husband had the secret of immortality. He had been given a magic potion by one of the gods and one day Heng O found it and drank it. All of a sudden she became weightless and flew out of the window.

When Sheng I came in, he saw that his wife was flying up to the moon and guessed what she had done. He tried to follow her but a hurricane blew up and lifted him to the palace of the god of the immortals. It was this god who gave Sheng I the sun to live in.

Heng O has lived in the moon ever since, in a beautiful palace made of precious gems, called The Palace of Great Cold. On the fifteenth day of every month, Sheng I flies from the sun to the moon on rays of light and visits his wife. That is why the moon is so bright at that time.

But some say that Sheng I was so angry with Heng O for stealing the potion of immortality that he changed her into a three-legged toad, which we can see in the moon to this day.

Moonlore

The moon is traditionally cold and frosty, by contrast with the hot sun, as you can read in the Fire-dogs story. It is also seen as mysterious and unobtainable, even though we know that humans have now walked on its surface. There are lots of sayings and beliefs connected with the moon.

If you take your money out and turn it over by the light of a new moon it will double in the course of the month.

Because the phases of the moon made it look as if it was filling up with water and emptying again, people used to believe that picking herbs or plants at full moon would mean they would be specially juicy and good.

The Anglo-Saxons had a different name for the moon according to each month – Wolf moon was January, Meadow Moon, July, Blood Moon was November, and so on. And there are hundreds of Native North American names for the moon from "Moon when the little lizard's tail freezes off" (January) to "Moon when cherries are ripe" (July).

One legend says that the moon is where all wasted time, broken promises, intentions that never turn into actions and unfulfilled desires end up. Alexander Pope the poet wrote that the moon was the home of all lost things, such as the brains of heroes and the tears of people hoping to inherit a dying person's money!

The hare in the moon

For the Hindus, the markings on the moon appear to be a hare. They explain that this was a brave animal who offered himself as dinner to the god Sakkira and was placed in the moon as a reward.

But there is another story about a hare who used his moonbrother to his advantage. It happened during a time of drought in India. There was a large herd of elephants, who were desperate for water to bathe in. All they could find was a little mud-puddle not big enough for one of them to sit in. So their leader, Shilimukha, went to scout around and found a beautiful lake full of clear water, just over the hill.

Down went the hot and dusty elephants stamping and trumpeting and crashing into the cool water. They didn't notice all the hares that lived on the edge of the lake, and many of them were trampled and killed.

The hares gathered round their leader, Vijaya, and asked him what to do. "These thirsty elephants are never going to go away now they've found our lake," they said, "and if they carry on like this we shall all die."

"Leave it to me," said Vijaya, but he didn't feel as brave as he sounded. He kept thinking of how much smaller he was than an elephant. That night he loped to the top of the hill and called out to Shilimukha, the elephant chief.

"Hear me, mighty one," he cried out. "I am an ambassador for the owner of this lake."

"And who is that?" asked Shilimukha, unimpressed.

"You can see him in the lake," said Vijaya, pointing to the reflection of the moon. "My master is angry. See how he trembles with rage in the water. We hares are his servants and guardians of the moonlake. That is why you see one of us in his beautiful face. He doesn't want his lake churned up by a lot of muddy elephants!"

Shilimukha was horrified. "We didn't know," he said. "We will go elsewhere to find water." And he made the herd go down on their knees.

"Forgive these foolish animals, master," said Vijaya solemnly, looking at the moon's reflection. "They didn't mean to insult you."
And he went back to the other hares, well pleased with himself.

54

Moonchildren

When the Norse gods made sun and moon out of fire-flakes from Muspel, the land of fire, they needed someone to drive their chariots across the sky. There was a mortal man called Mundilfari who had two children who were very beautiful. So proud was Mundilfari of his children that he named his daughter Sol, which means Sun, and his son Mani, which means Moon.

To punish him for giving the names of heavenly bodies to human children, the gods took Sol and Mani and made them the charioteers of the Sun and Moon. They are both chased by monstrous wolves across the sky.

The wolf who chases Mani is called Hati, the Hater, and he is a giant in disguise. Every night he chases handsome Mani through the heavens, always hoping to swallow him up. If Hati ever does catch up with Mani and devour him, the heavens and the earth willl turn red with blood. It will be a sign of the end of the world.

But Mani is not alone on his nightly journey. He has two companions, a girl and a boy, and this is how he got them. There was a man called Vidfinn who sent his two children, Hyuki and Bil, out at night to bring some water from a magic spring on a mountain-top. This spring was full of the liquid which inspired poetry and prophecy.

Off went Hyuki and Bil with their bucket and dipped it into the spring till it was full. They raised it up on a pole, spilling some of the precious liquid and attracting Mani's attention. As they were going down the mountain, he reached down and scooped them up into his chariot, bucket, pole and all.

You can still see the boy, the girl, the bucket and the pole in the moon and poets call out to Bil the beautiful, begging her to sprinkle their lips with the magic springwater.

The cheese in the pond

There was a village in England long ago, in Nottinghamshire, as a matter of fact, where all the people were very foolish. They were famous for it, so famous that they were known as "the wise people of Gotham", which meant quite the opposite.

Just to show you how foolish they were, once upon a time a woman of Gotham was walking home from her neighbour's one night when she spotted something large and round and pale in the horse-pond.

"Come quickly!" she shouted. "There's a cheese in the pond. Fetch nets and rakes!"

She woke her husband, who came running, and so did many other villagers. They stared at the big round cheese in the pond. They threw their nets to catch it and they dug in their rakes to scoop it. They tried and tried all night, but no-one could get the cheese out of the pond.

When dawn broke the tired villagers looked into the water and there was nothing there but mud and weeds.

"It must have been eaten by a big fish while we weren't looking," said the woman and all the villagers nodded their heads in agreement. You see why they were known as "The Wise People of Gotham"!

STARS

Aries

The ram with the golden fleece, which was the object of the journey of Jason and the Argonauts. Originally the ram carried a hero called Phrixus away from his stepmother Ino who wanted to kill him. When Phrixus arrived safely in Colchis he sacrificed the ram and hung its fleece in the grove of the war god Ares, where it turned to gold.

Taurus

The origin of this constellation's symbol can be claimed by many mythological bulls. The Egyptians worshipped Osiris as a bull-god, the Greeks identified this constellation with the white bull that Europa fell in love with, who was Zeus in disguise, and for the Persians, the death of a bull was an important part of the rituals that celebrated the arrival of spring. The Pleiades are a star cluster in Taurus.

Gemini

The twin constellation representing Castor and Polydeuces, the sons of Leda by Zeus, when he disguised himself as a swan. The Romans saw them as Romulus and Remus. There are stories about heavenly twins in many cultures.

Cancer

The crab who pinched Hercules' toes while he was struggling with the Hydra. Hercules stamped on it and Hera placed it in the sky. The Babylonians saw it as a tortoise, and the Chaldeans thought it was the gate through which souls descended from heaven into human bodies.

Leo

This was the Nemean lion, killed by Hercules, who continued to wear the lionskin afterwards, as a symbol of his bravery and because it was supposed to protect against all weapons.

Virgo

This constellation has been identified with every important female figure, from Ishtar, the Phoenician love goddess, to the Greek Persephone, to the Virgin Mary. Sometimes she is seen as Dike, the Greek goddess of justice, because of her position in relation to Libra, the scales, the traditional emblem of just and equal measurement.

Libra

Libra wasn't always treated as a separate constellation; it used to be the claws of Scorpio. Now it stands for the equinox, when night and day are balanced at the same length.

Scorpio

This is the insect who killed the hunter Orion by stinging him in the foot. The constellation is at the opposite end of the sky from Orion's. But the identification of this constellation as a scorpion goes back to the Sumerians more than 5000 years ago.

Sagittarius

This constellation has been shown as a centaur since classical times. But there is another constellation called Centaurus and this has led to confusion. It may be Crotus, the satyr, who invented archery.

Capricorn

Oriental legends make this the nurse of the young sun-god. It was a she-goat with a fish's tail. The Greeks saw it as the hairy goat-shaped god Pan, who disguised part of himself as a fish when he was helping Zeus escape from the monster Typhon.

Aquarius

A man or boy pouring water out of an urn, frequently identified with Ganymede the immortal cupbearer to the gods on Olympus.

Pisces

The Babylonian, Syriac, Persian and Turkish names for this constellation all translate as "fish". The Greeks thought these two fishes were Aphrodite and her son Eros. The legend was that they had changed themselves into fishes and dived into the Euphrates river when they were being chased by the monster Typhon.

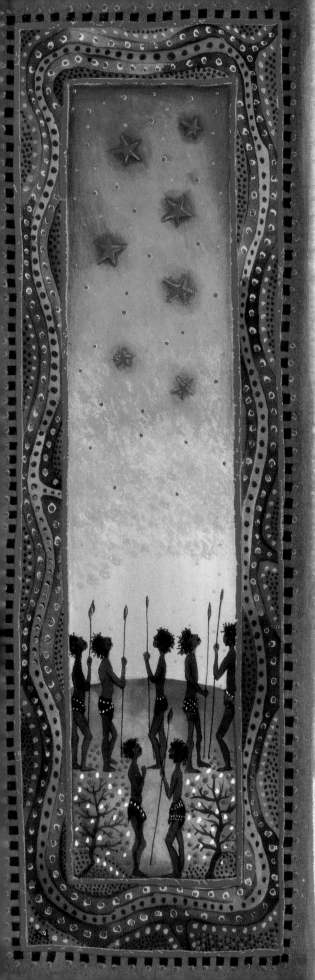

Seven sisters

There were seven beautiful sisters who lived the life of hunters. They were called the Meamei and they all had waist-length hair and their bodies sparkled with icicles. They were like a long drink of ice-cold water in the hot country where they lived.

They never joined other groups when they hunted, but there was a family of brothers called the Berai-Berai who admired the sisters' beauty and wanted to marry them. The Berai-Berai were very good at finding honey and used to leave sweet honeycombs outside the camp of the Meamei. The lovely women ate the honey, laughing, and wouldn't listen when their admirers talked of marriage.

There was a much more dangerous suitor after them. The Fiery Ancestor, Wurrunnah, laid an ambush and caught the Meamei. But even he must have found seven strong hunters hard to handle, because he took five of them and put them in the sky. He kept two for a while, trying to warm the icicles off them, but only succeeded in putting out his own fire.

After many struggles the two escaped from Wurrunnah and joined their sisters in the sky. But if you look up at the Pleiades, which is what the Meamei became, you will see that two are dimmer than the rest. Those are the two sisters whose icy sparkle was dimmed by Wurrunnah's fiery embrace.

The Berai-Berai were devastated by the loss of the beautiful Meamei and wouldn't consider marrying any other young women. They refused to eat and pined away, looking up at the seven stars. After their death the spirits took pity on them and now the young men can also be seen in the night sky. In the north, they are known as the belt and sword of Orion, but the Australian aborigines still call them the Berai-Berai.

The Berai-Berai still go hunting for honey among the stars and the Meamei sing evening songs to them from their camp. In the cold time they sometimes break off bits of ice from themselves and throw them down to earth. When the aborigines see morning frost they know that the Meamei have not forgotten them. And when it thunders, they say it is the Meamei jumping into water, playing at who can make the loudest splash. Then they know that rain is on the way.

The divided lovers

Tentei, the King of the Stars, had one beautiful daughter, whose name was Orihime. Princess Orihime was very clever at weaving and could make the most wonderful clothes. Her father was proud of her but he kept her so busy weaving that she never had time to do anything else. Orihime's heart was heavy, because she thought she would never meet anyone and fall in love.

At last her father took pity on her and chose her a husband. Kengyu was a cowherd who lived across the river. Orihime and Kengyu got married and were blissfully happy, so happy that Orihime left her loom to gather dust and made no more beautiful clothes.

Tentei was angry. He thought that Orihime was neglecting her work. He decided to separate the two lovers and make them live on opposite banks of the great river. Now, this was no ordinary river, because it ran through the kingdom of the stars. It was the Milky Way. Orihime and Kengyu had no way to cross it.

Orihime missed Kengyu so much she wept until her tears ran over the cloth she was weaving.

"You'll stain the cloth!" said Tentei. "Very well. If you miss your husband so much, you can see him once a year."

So the King of the Stars arranged that once a year, on the seventh day of the seventh month, the boatman of the moon comes to ferry Orihime across the river to visit Kengyu.

But if the princess doesn't do her weaving properly, Tentei makes it rain so hard that the river floods and the boatman won't come. When this happens, all the magpies in Japan fly to the river and form a bridge so that Orihime steps lightly over their feathered backs to reach her beloved Kengyu.

And there is nothing her father can do about it.

Starlore

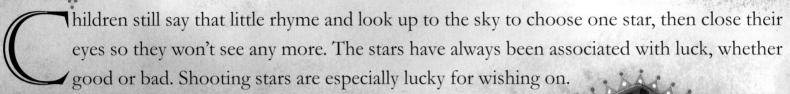

Starlight, starbright,
First star I see tonight.
I wish I may, I wish I might,
Have the wish I wish tonight.

Children still say that little rhyme and look up to the sky to choose one star, then close their eyes so they won't see any more. The stars have always been associated with luck, whether good or bad. Shooting stars are especially lucky for wishing on.

There are lots of stories featuring the morning star and the evening stars as rivals or partners. In fact they are both the same – the planet Venus.

There is an ancient Hindu ritual in which a newly-married man could not speak to his bride until the stars came out. As soon as he saw the Pole Star, he would point it out to her and call on it to make sure his wife would be loyal and faithful to him.

The most famous star of all is the Star of Bethlehem which led the three wise men to Jesus' birthplace in a stable. These wise men were probably astronomers and their modern equivalents have worked out that the "star of wonder" may have been a triple conjunction of Jupiter, Saturn and the stars of the constellation Pisces.

The price of vanity

If you live in the Northern hemisphere, one of the easiest constellations to identify is Cassiopeia. It looks like a huge letter W written in stars. To the ancient Greeks, it looked like the figure of a woman and they linked it with the story of Cassiopeia, Andromeda and Perseus.

Cassiopeia was a very vain woman, always brushing her long hair and admiring herself in the mirror. She was queen of Ethiopia and married to King Cepheus. One day she boasted that she was more beautiful than the Nereids, the fifty lovely sea nymphs. This was not a wise move, because one of the Nereids was the wife of Poseidon, powerful god of the sea, and she complained to him about Cassiopeia's boast.

Poseidon sent a sea-serpent to ravage the coast of Ethiopia. The people were terrified by the monster and begged their king to do something about it so Cepheus sent for advice to an oracle. The oracle's advice horrified him. The only way to make the monster go away was to chain his lovely daughter Andromeda to the rocks and give her to the serpent. How sorry Cassiopeia was for her silly boasting when she saw her daughter weeping on the rocks while the monster came churning through the waves towards her!

Just then Perseus came flying through the sky with his winged sandals. He was a great hero, on his way back from killing the Medusa – but that's another story. He took one look at the beautiful young woman chained to the rocks and fell in love. He swooped down and killed the sea-monster with his diamond sword and claimed the grateful Andromeda as his wife.

Now all the characters in this story are remembered in the stars. Andromeda lies between Cassiopeia and Perseus. King Cepheus's stars are near his wife's and even the monster can be seen, as the constellation Cetus. According to tradition, Cassiopeia is still combing her hair and spends part of the year upside down as a punishment for her vanity.

White Star Woman and Great Star

Tirawa, the One Above, made the stars. And the two most important were White Star Woman, who was the Evening star, and Great Star, who was the Morning star. Everything that came about in the world was to come from the union of these two stars.

But first Great Star had to win White Star Woman for his wife and he set out to seek her in her home in the West, but White Star Woman saw him coming and put many obstacles in his path. Ten times she blocked his way with floods or thorn forests or monsters and ten times Great Star took a ball of fire from his pocket and hurled it at the hindrance till it burned up and disappeared.

At last he came near to White Star Woman's house. It was guarded by a black bear, a mountain-lion, a wild-cat and a wolf. These were no ordinary beasts but were stars themselves. They were also a promise of all the animals that were to come to be on the earth and of the weather, the trees and the life-giving corn.

Great Star put them in their places, making them the four quarters of the world and giving them charge of the four seasons.

White Star Woman saw that her marriage with Great Star was meant to be. But first she made him do three things. She told him to bring her a cradle-board for their first child, a soft rug to lay it on and some sweet fresh water to bathe it in.

Great Star brought her a cradle-board patterned with stars, a rug made from the softest part of a buffalo-hide and water from a fresh spring bordered with sweet-smelling grasses. So White Star Woman consented to become Great Star's wife and each gave to the other all the powers that were within them. White Star Woman dropped a pebble from the heavens which became the Earth and Great Star threw his ball of fire into the sky where it became the Sun.

Their daughter was placed on a cloud and sent gently down to earth carrying the blessing of corn with her. She dropped from the cloud like rain and met a boy who was the child of the Sun and Moon. From these two came all the people who live on the earth. And Tirawa, the Unchanging, gave the stars the duty of watching over all people. When they die, their spirits climb the Milky Way and go to live for ever in the stars.

The giant's skull

Stories of the creation of the world in Norse mythology are found in prose and poetry of twelfth-century Iceland. A good reference collection is Kevin Crossley-Holland's *Norse Myths* (Deutsch 1980). Roger Lancelyn Green's *Myths of the Norsemen* (Puffin 1970) is still a good version for younger readers.

Mother Sky

Egyptian mythology can be very confusing, because of the many sacred texts and inscriptions found which relate to different time periods and geographical regions. A useful guide is George Hart *Egyptian Myths* (British Museum Press 1990).

A handful of quartz

This account of the origin of heavenly bodies is taken from Franc Johnson Newcomb's *Navaho Folk Tales* (University of New Mexico Press 1967).

War in heaven

There is no convenient source in English for Baltic mythology but there is a useful summary of the main stories in Janet McCrickard's *Eclipse of the Sun* (Gothic Image 1990).

The king's fire dogs

This explanation of eclipses of the sun and moon comes from Zong In-Sob's *Folk Tales from Korea* (Routledge 1952). The Hindu explanation, involving the demons Rahu and Ketu can be found in W.J.Wilkins *Hindu Mythology* (Rupa & Co 1975).

SUN

The heavenly archer

This account of the exploits of Sheng I comes from *Ancient Tales and Folklore of China* by Edward T.C. Warner (Studio Editions 1995).

When the sun hid

The story of Amaterasu, the Shinto sun goddess, can be found in F.Hadland Davis *Myths and Legends of Japan* (Dover 1992). I've taken the spellings and some detail from McCrickard 1990.

The fifth sun

Both Mayan and Aztec mythologies have stories of the five worlds and their suns. This version is based on *Aztec and Maya Myths* Karl Taube (British Museum Press 1993).

In the sun's house

I've consulted several sources on Navajo mythology and ceremonial but the main points of this re-telling come from Maud Oakes and Joseph Campbell's *Where the two came to their father* (Princeton University Press 1943, rev 1991).

Phaëton's last ride

The story of Phaëton's chariot, which even gave its name to an elegant carriage in Regency England, is well known throughout the Western world. You can find it in Robert Graves *The Greek Myths* (Penguin 1992).

MOON

Anancy and the Flipflap bird

This is a story of the Caribbean trickster, which originated in Ghana. I found it on the Internet in *Folktales from the World.* (http://www.ucalgary.ca/~dkbrown/storfolk.html)

The drowned moon

This story was first recorded in 1891 and you can find a version of it in Joseph Jacobs *English Fairy Tales* (re-issued Bodley Head 1968).

The woman who flew to the moon

This story of Heng O is a companion to the heavenly archer in the "Sun" section. I used *Ancient Tales and Folklore of China* by Edward T.C. Warner (Studio Editions 1995).

The hare in the moon

The first story alluded to can be found, along with lots of other moon stories in *Moonlore* by Gwydion O'Hara (Lelwellyn Publications USA 1996). The story of the elephants and the hares comes from the Hitopadesha in the version by J.E.B. Gray *Indian Myths and Legends* (OUP 1961).

Moonchildren

The story is found in Snorri Sturlusson's "Deluding of Gylfi" in *The Prose Edda* (CUP 1954). It was suggested by S. Baring-Gould in 1866 that Hyuki and Bil were the originals of the nursery rhyme characters Jack and Jill. See Iona & Peter Opie's *Oxford Dictionary of Nursery Rhymes* (OUP 1951).

The cheese in the pond

Stories of The Wise Men of Gotham abound in English folktale collections. You can find this one in Kevin Crossley-Holland's *British Folk Tales* (Orchard Books 1987).

STARS

The circle of beasts

Most of the information in this section comes from
R.H.Allen's *Starnames, their lore and meaning* (Dover 1963) or
Ian Ridpath's *Star Tales* (Lutterworth 1988).

Seven sisters

From *More Australian Legendary Tales* by K. Langloh Parker
(David Nutt 1898).

The divided lovers

Orihime is Vega, the brightest star in the Lyra constellation.
Kengyu is Altair, the alpha star of the Aquila constellation.
This story came to Japan from China in the late part of the
7th century AD. See Megumi Hara *Seiza no Shinwa*
(Mythology of the Constellations) (Kouseisha Co. Ltd
1980). I have added the reference to Orihime's tears.

The price of vanity

This story can be found in Robert Graves *Greek Myths*
(Penguin 1992). To see what these and other constellations
look like *The Box of Stars* by Catherine Tennant (Chatto &
Windus 1993) is very helpful.

White Star Woman and Great Star

This myth was told to Natalie Curtis by Sakuruta of the
Morning-Star Clan and reproduced in *The Indians' Book*
(Bonanza Books 1906, republished 1987).

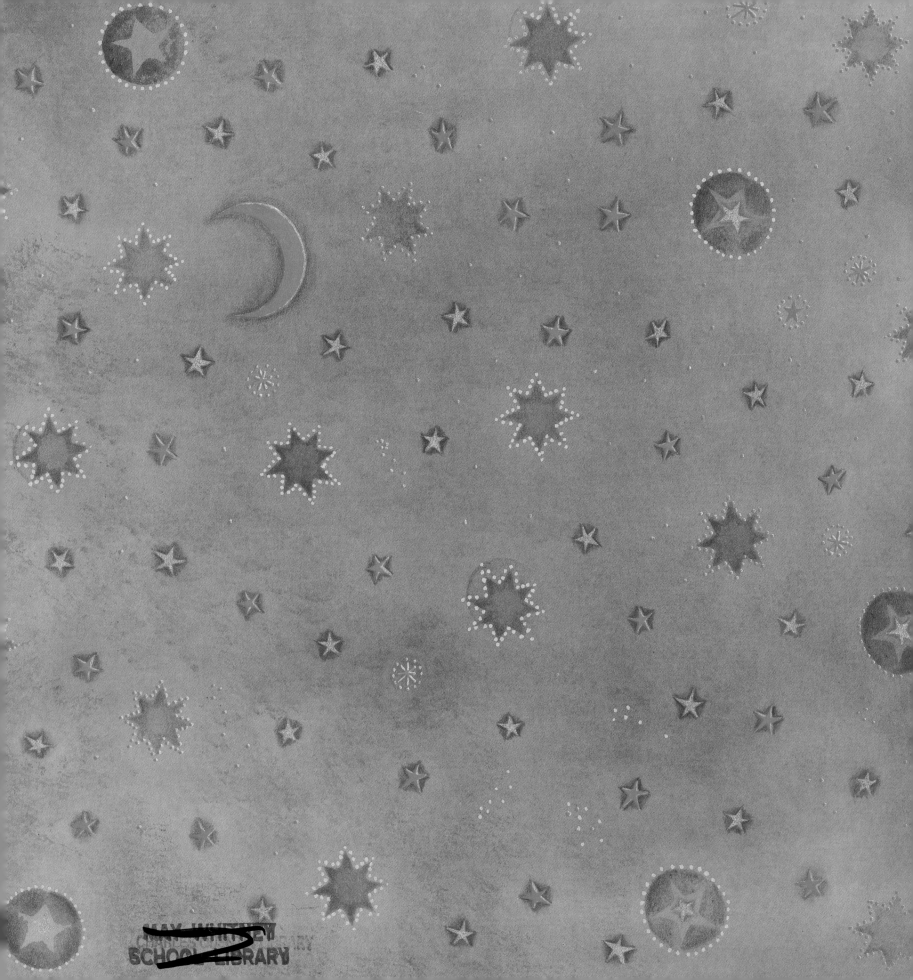